Everyday Beliefs

Paperback ISBN: 979-8-88590-554-1
eBook ISBN: 979-8-88590-555-8

Everyday Beliefs

Dan Johnson

PREFACE

This is the protocol I've developed to significantly reduce and inactivate epidermolysis bullosa (EB) simplex in my body.

I am writing this book to be of assistance to the EB community (which encompasses the friends and families of EB-gifted folks) as well as the doctors that treat EB, which is a rare connective tissue disorder that causes the skin to blister and tear easily. There are various types of EB, some of which are more severe and sometimes fatal. It is estimated that EB has a prevalence of about 500,000 people worldwide according to EB Research Network. I have extensive firsthand knowledge of EB, as I was born with it and have lived with it for most of my life. The second half of my life will be without it by choice. EB inactivation is the only area that I have mastered—for now. With that being said, I have so much more to learn and research about EB prevention and elimination. I see this book as the start of my work, not the end. I look forward to the day when the entire EB community and their families will be free of all the heartaches and headaches that it can bring into their lives, as there are many.

A note for the doctors treating people with EB: This is a guide to take EB from being an unpreventable or unknown problem to a manageable condition by embracing, experimenting with, and implementing the guide into your practice. I encourage you to be brave and try all or some of the practices and products that I outline in this protocol, which continues to provide me with a blister-free life. In addition,

I encourage you to prescribe the very best nutritional plan possible to your patients. It will take time to figure out which foods work best for which people. But you will be able to gather enough information from this protocol and your own investigative work to determine a good foundation that can be applied to most patients. I am here for you. I am willing to be your helper, adviser, and recommendation giver if you are willing to listen. I have lived with EB for almost thirty years. I know what your patients are going through, day in and day out. I also know what families with children that have EB are going through. I will make myself available to you. The only way that we will completely eliminate this will be through collaboration.

For the folks with EB: Your job is to always see the positive in your situation and use it to your advantage. Have the courage not only to try different products but also to see your problem from a different perspective. Above all, have patience with yourself, the doctors, and all the manufacturers out there that make products that will someday be of valuable help to you. For all the products I list throughout this book, I'm sure there are alternatives that may taste better, fit better, work better for you, or be more within your budget. Experiment, and have fun doing so. And know this: it's a starting point for you, and your results can only get better from here.

For the families of EB children: You, too, have a very big role to play in this—more than you know. I urge you to encourage your children to experiment with anything they can think of that may help them. It's all too easy to tell them to sit on the couch or not to go out because it's too hot. After all, you are the ones that have to listen to the complaining, see the pain, and in some cases, provide the aftercare for all the wounds. This is a process that you have to take an active part in. Better days are ahead for sure. I am here for you as well. Use me as a resource. It would be an honor to help you and your loved ones.

Dan Johnson   vii

TABLE OF CONTENTS

CHAPTER 1

The Start of My EB Journey

I grew up in Dedham, Massachusetts, a young boy that loved to play, ride bikes, and walk, like every other kid—when I could. I suffered from EB; that's how I viewed it at that age: suffered. Epidermolysis bullosa is a rare problem that affected just about everything I did or wanted to do. Later, after reading and learning about EB, I would classify mine as between EB Simplex and Junctional EB according to Cincinnati Childrens.org. But it's difficult to say. I would have to study them all in great detail to put a more accurate label on myself.

EB was passed down to me from my mother's side of the family. My brother, my mother, my grandmother, my uncle, and his kids—we've all had it passed down to us. We've lived with it and dealt with it as best we could. As a child I tried to hide it and not tell anyone about it out of fear of rejection or embarrassment. But you can't hide the limping and the wounds on your hands, legs, or feet, especially at the beach! If I sat too close to a campfire, then I'd end up getting blisters on my face! I remember not participating in any outdoor hot-weather activities in my school years. Even when playing hockey or skiing in the winter, I blistered, sometimes heavily. I would blister like crazy playing street hockey in the summer: on my hands, on my feet, on my armpits, and even around my crotch. If the body part rubbed on something or sweated, then I seemed to blister there. From what I understand, other forms of EB can be far worse, even lethal. I guess I am lucky; at least I could run and play in the summer, even if only for ten to twenty minutes before I blistered to the point of needing to go home and sit down.

For the first fifteen years or so of my life, I played the victim. How could I have been born with this? Why did I live in Boston, where the summers were scorching hot and humid? I was not enjoying my life to the fullest. Back then I wanted to live in Canada because it was always cold up there. I said to myself, when I'm old enough to move, I will move to Canada. I'm glad that didn't happen. If I had moved to a colder region of the world, then it would not have led me to develop better ways to live, enjoying life in the hot areas that the world has to offer. Now I live in Florida, where it is always hot. This is beneficial: I can further advance my study of EB, as it is a perfect training ground for me—or anyone with

EB. What better way is there to test products, daily practices, and mindsets?

I started playing hockey around the age of four. Those skates really hurt me initially, but over time by wearing them in the house off and on, my skin got a little tougher, and the skates broke in until I could skate in them for an hour. I'm glad my uncle Paul got me involved in the sport. It taught me many things about myself that I applied later in life to create a protocol for inactivating blisters. With my protocol I can perform any sport at any time in any climate, wearing any gear on my feet, hands, and body.

In my late teens and early twenties, I took up skiing as this was a nice cool-weather sport, good for the skin. I blistered so badly that I could do only about three runs before I was done. I would force myself to do half a day and ruin my shins, meaning, they would be covered completely in blisters. It would take more than a week to heal. Of all places, I never got blisters on my shins as I've never had to work my shins in any other activities before. Playing hockey, I learned a trick: buying my own boots rather than wearing rentals. This gave my body the ability to adapt to the boots' pressure points (your body is unable to adapt to a different pair of boots every time you ski). Just as I once did with my skates, I would wear them around the house off and on, for longer and longer. I would even mimic skiing, making the same moves on the carpet in the house as I would on the snow on the mountain. The more I did this, the tougher my skin got. I was able to ski for longer. By the end of a ski season, I could ski all weekend—three-day weekends, even. I loved skiing so much that it became a passion. I skied every weekend and all over the world. My shins would always get one or two blisters from wearing ski boots, though it happened less and less.

I always enjoyed après-ski, and this, I learned, was a big problem. Alcohol and EB are a really bad combination that will bring about blisters and swelling on the spot or the day after drinking. Once I eliminated drinking while on ski trips, zero blisters! I added that to my protocol. I would drink only on my last day there, after the day of skiing. That way I had the long four-hour drive home the next day to rest my body and skin. By keeping a positive attitude, trying different products and practices, and staying persistent, I collected the big payout of no blisters while skiing for up to a week at a time, even after some of my friends without EB were too beat up to ski another day. Not me.

Now, let's try all these methods on a summer sport!

I made the choice to get involved with cycling around the age of twenty-four. I saw a mountain bike go by one day and thought, boy, that looks really fun. So I bought one, got on it, and rode for about half an hour. This blistered my hands and ass really badly, but my feet, not so badly. I purchased dedicated riding shoes and wearing them around the house until they were broken in, and my skin adapted. With no alcohol the night before, I would ride my bike a bit longer each time after my body recovered enough to do it. It could have been every day or every other day, depending on the severity of the blisters. Regardless, the blisters would pop, and I could feel the pain, but I continued to ride.

I would retreat to the blister pad (a clean face cloth with a sterilized needle to pop blisters), recover for four or five days, then repeat. I started applying hand cream before a ride, which made a big difference. Then I discovered a Hammer Nutrition product called Seat Saver. Game changer for my ass! I applied this to my butt wherever it would come in contact with the seat. I can't say enough about this product and the positive effect it had on my cycling career. I also purchased and wore very high-quality bibs from Hammer Nutrition with built-in pads that were thin, comfortable, and didn't cause any blisters. Bibs are a typical "uniform" that a cyclist will wear. Like a football player wearing shoulder pads and spandex, a cyclist will wear a bib or shorts with a built-in saddle pad for comfort.

I then bought a road bike and started riding all day in the summer heat. I built up my skin, body, mind, spirit, and muscles to take back-to-back century rides (one hundred miles) in Boston and Pennsylvania every summer. On average I was riding five hundred miles a week, regardless of temperature, with not a single blister to be found. I was blown away. Did I defeat this?

I started thinking about how I was able to do this. It was a miracle to me. But I could see that my protocol, built through trial and error, was working. I was eliminating all the negative programming from my childhood. I was finally getting into my subconscious mind, and it was delivering my dream. Believing is seeing! I cycled from my early to mid-twenties to the age of approximately thirty-seven years old, consistently, with great success. My longest run without a single blister is five years, and this was during the height of my cycling career.

Staying active is important for body, mind, and spirit. Our bodies were made to move, not to sit for extended periods of time. This is something I see my relatives do, and more often than not, they have blisters and can't go out or do much.

I got married at the age of forty, and life began to change organically. We ended up getting a lot of dogs and buying a horse farm in Connecticut, and I slowly dropped bits and pieces of my protocol. After about two years, I was following only the hydration portion and some of the nutrition. All my blister problems began to surface again, sometimes pretty badly. They were slowing me down or causing me to sit on the couch. I can remember a few vacations when I had to take it easy. I really don't like taking it easy. I'll do that after they bury me.

Fast-forward to age fifty. We sold the horse farm and bought a smaller horse farm in Ocala, Florida. My wife moved to Ocala, but I still had to find a job down south before I could join her, and the horse farm sold so fast that I had no place to live. So I moved in with a friend of mine in Dedham. I was about forty pounds overweight and once again having trouble with blisters. They weren't so bad because I was taking it easy due to my obesity and lack of motivation. Fed up with how I looked in the mirror and blisters coming and going, I wanted my energy and vitality back. I decided to pull out the old protocol to see if it would work. With laser focus, in just three months, I was almost blister-free and dropped 30 pounds of body fat. and I was becoming more and more active. I was also pushing myself to greater challenges, such as difficult hikes and trail running. I figured out that I could turn the symptoms of EB off and on at my discretion.

Not long afterward I began documenting all that I had done to get there and really thinking about how I did it. I realized I had become unconsciously competent. I couldn't explain how I did it or train someone else to do it. I couldn't provide any instructions. But after I documented a good amount of information, what was important and what wasn't became clear to me. I had to think back to my childhood. There were a lot of "oh, yeah" moments as I relived my past.

Growing up, I went to many doctors, some of them specializing in dermatology or EB. They could feel sad for me; they could feed me more bad advice (not intentionally, of course); they could administer a whole host of chemicals to my body or throw them down my gullet. I have something to tell you—and this is just my opinion—but if the doctor you or your children see doesn't have EB, then they probably will not be able to deliver superior results.

If the end result is picking up the newest chemical, antibiotic or pill, then that, they can achieve. In my opinion, from experience, most of the doctors that I visited or were referred to were not trained in nutrition or the mind, let alone EB. Even those that are very knowledgeable about why we get EB provide treatments that basically amount to "sit down in a cool room and take it easy." They made every attempt to treat me with a prescription or advice that didn't fit my life, let alone prevent or inactivate my EB.

I often wondered why I went to someone who doesn't have EB to look for advice or help. This seems like backward logic to me now. I guess I thought that they went to school for these things and could provide the best possible answers. Now I believe that people with EB know best. I eventually inactivated EB on my own because I wasn't satisfied with what the doctors were selling or the results I was getting. By all means if you have excellent results with the doctor you are seeing, then stick with them. I am happy you have found one that can deliver. We are a group of special people who need special products, special mindsets and attitudes, special foods, and so on.

When I was growing up, the only people with EB that I knew were in my family. They followed the standard American diet and didn't push themselves or their minds. There was one exception: my uncle Paul. Thank you, Paul, for getting me involved with hockey and pushing my mind to overcome. It has paid massive dividends in my life.

By holding on to a vision of being blister-free through many years of trial and error, my protocol has completely in-activated blisters in my day-to-day life. I will spell it all out for you in detail. Feel free to play with it and create your own that works for you. Some things are negotiable or ad-justable for me and possibly you, such as portion sizes and the colors of the footwear products I recommend. But some things are nonnegotiable for me, such as nutrition, hydration, good socks, and controlling my thoughts, reprogramming my subconscious mind to Eliminate Beliefs that hold me back. You can implement all that I lay out in the protocol and will achieve a great level of success. But if you don't master your mind and use certain items and foods, you will not achieve total success—just my opinion, built on many years of experience. I have played with this protocol up, down, and sideways, in many variations, and I still am. I have hurt myself at times, experimenting with a host of things. This is part of the success and steering process. I was also hurting myself by taking prescription pills and chemicals when I was younger. Think of the long-term effects that would have had on me.

I have also spent a fortune on books, products, and foods from around the world in an effort to inactivate my EB. I will continue to do so. I will never stop improving my position in all areas of my life. My next goal with EB is elimination. I'm already halfway there! I have inactivation mastered. I can turn EB on or off at will, like a light switch. This took years to accomplish. One might ask if I can turn it off, then why would I turn it back on? As many of you know, life happens. I just recently went through a divorce and have been drinking alcohol more than I should. This is causing my feet and hands issues. Sometimes I get caught up in a good time with friends and do not adhere to eating correctly or drinking alcohol excessively. The protocol I created and follow to turn the blisters off is strict and must be adhered to 100 percent for proper results. If I follow it 80 percent, then 80 percent will be my result. I am glad that I stopped following the protocol a few years back as it led me to write it all out to help you and others. It has been successfully implemented in my life twice with outstanding results. I have tried to recruit family members to follow my protocol, but they are stuck in the paradigm that they have EB and that nothing can be done except to sit and relax or take the drugs and chemicals the doctors are pushing. They, my family, also refer to me as a quack. Funny, since they are the ones using harsh chemicals and antidepressants, chain-smoking, and popping pills instead of living full lives!

With the right mindset and products, life is so much better. I hope that people who start thinking this way will find even more positive-result products that can make a difference in our lives. I am counting on you to implement some or all of my protocol and report back the positive benefits you experience. Maybe you can share tricks of the trade with me that I don't know yet. I have found that following my protocol delivers better results than any doctor has delivered, with or without EB experience. I encourage everyone that reads this to follow their own intuition, imagination, and willpower to take it all into their own hands.

A message to the doctors getting marginal results at best: implement some or all of this protocol with a patient, and after six documented months—well, you tell me. I believe this protocol will shift your EB treatment to a preventative practice with your patients. In addition, you'll save them and yourselves a great deal of time and money. I can't tell you how much money I have forked over in co-pays for chemicals and pills that doctors thought might help. Not to mention the countless hours of sitting in waiting rooms and filling out forms.

There is a great book called *Doctor, Your Medicine Is Killing Me!* by Pete Coussa. This book will introduce you to alternative medicine and taking charge of your ailments. He has a disease model that shows how stress or any negative emotion, fast food, sugar, and soda create problems with the body's organs. I will be mentioning great books often, as they have helped me get to where I am today. I even read them a second time and discover another lesson, something else to try that I missed or forgot the first time. Reading and research have been instrumental in the development of my protocol to prevent and inactivate EB. I crave information and new products. I'm always searching online or asking people about products they use. It's an insatiable appetite for a better quality of life and the ability to push myself to higher levels of performance. I do believe that, in the future, advancements in gene and cell therapy may provide a cure—or at the very least, great advancements—for people with EB. I worked in the pharmaceutical industry for over twelve years, and I have seen the work being done to advance these types of therapies for various diseases.

I do have two addictions at the moment: living life without EB and coffee, black and hot. Coffee is something that I have had a very difficult time eliminating. I am addicted to it and crave it upon waking up. I have a cup midday as well, though I can live without the midday cup. I eliminated all other addictions years ago. These include cigarettes, heavy drinking, pot smoking, and hanging with the wrong crowd. My occasional enjoyments now, which do have a negative effect on my blisters, are cigars, bourbon and red wine. But I can live without them, too, and I use them as celebratory allowances. They are not healthy, but I allow myself to enjoy them once in a while, usually after accomplishing something great—a ten-hour hike, a century ride—or after going through something hard, such as the passing of a loved one. I love red wine and will enjoy a glass or two over dinner. There is a lot of sugar in red wine, so I have cut back on it recently. A shot of high-quality whiskey or bourbon does the trick now.

What I'm going to share with you is the most current regimen I follow. I'm not offering medical advice. I'm not going to ask you to apply chemicals to your skin or take pills that block one thing from working correctly to make something else work correctly. These are simple methods, mindsets, attitudes, and clothing and nutrition practices to use in your own way. You can pick and choose what you want to implement. My only wish is that this protocol might greatly improve the life of someone with EB. If anyone is able to achieve inactivation of their EB, as I have, that will be a complete success.

I'm filled with gratitude to be able to share this information, which will help you in many ways. If you have purchased this book, you are on the right track. You want and deserve a better life for yourself or someone with EB, and I'd like to personally thank you for letting me help. Even if you follow only half of this protocol, life will improve. It's all natural, with no co-pays or doctor visits (unless you decide to ask your doctor about nutritional changes), no forms to fill out or chemicals to apply to your body. It can all be done in your home, at your leisure and pace. By all means, take the time to do your own research on the products, foods, and practices that I recommend. This will only benefit you, strengthening your knowledge base on the subject and products. Check with your doctor before starting any of this, if you wish, though I did not. If I had checked with my doctor, then this book wouldn't be in front of you, and I would still be limping around in agony. I'm glad I stopped going to see so many doctors and so-called specialists. Just take an honest look at your results. That should tell you everything you need to know.

CHAPTER 2

My Career Choices

*Whether you think you can or you think you can't,
you're right.*

—Henry Ford

As far as my career went, I wanted to be an auto mechanic. My parents warned me that, with my feet and hands, there would be better choices. They were right. However, all the days when I came home in serious pain were the beginning of my long journey to creating this protocol, because I wouldn't settle for anything other than what I wanted to do. Working on hot engines with hand tools and wearing work boots in a shop that was not air-conditioned was a recipe for disaster! It took two or three years for my hands and feet to adapt. I'm so grateful that my boss did not fire me. I was out of work many days of the week in the summer. Now I work with hand tools all the time, and I love it.

I got out of auto mechanics and started working in robotics. This required me to wear steel-toed shoes for twelve hours at a time, again with no air-conditioning. This was what I called the next level of punishment for living. By three hours into the workday, I would be crippled and panicking about how to make it through the rest of the day. I would go home at the end of the day and soak my feet in chlorine and water, praying I could work the standard eight-hour day or the mandatory-overtime twelve-hour day the next day. I stressed out about this. I would slip my regular sneakers on and hope no one noticed. My boss did, though, and he told me to go put the steel-toes back on. He got mad after having to tell me this several times in one day. I explained to him that the boots were hurting my feet and causing a blister. He told me to buy another pair the next time the boot truck arrived. He wasn't kidding, the boot truck is an industrial footwear vehicle for large companies with employees in the hundreds or greater. Everyone gets a free or discounted pair of safety shoes. Everyone is allotted a time slot to go to the truck and try on shoes until he or she finds a pair of shoes that fit.

The next time the truck came in, I discovered steel-toed sneakers and bought a pair. I secretly drilled holes in the steel caps to let air go through. Eventually I stumbled upon the Good Feet Store. This is a national chain that helps people with foot pain. I stopped in at a local branch that caught my eye one day. I bought a pair of orthotic inserts, which slide into your shoes to help with high arches or flat feet. In my case, high arches. And I purchased their insoles that slide on top of the orthotics. These, coupled with my new sneakers and their drilled-out steel toes, were a quantum leap for my feet and my attitude. Persistence was paying off. I did not stop, and I won. Most people with EB or other disabilities would have quit if they had even taken the job in the first place, knowing they had to wear steel-toed boots. But I wanted that job badly enough that my mind created ways to overcome and adapt. I did not quit. This was one of the biggest pivot points in my life with EB. Afterward, I really began challenging what I had been brought up to be. Everyone has a defining moment that makes a massive difference. This was one of mine.

And it was easy. I just had to be willing to look into new products, spend the money, and not get disappointed when I had to throw away what didn't work or made things worse. In addition to suffering from EB, I have high arches, which create pressure points on my heels and the balls of my feet. But with Good Feet arch supports, the weight of my body was evenly distributed across my whole foot, not just the heel and the ball, providing a stable foot and a lot less blister-ing. After a year, I could walk in steel-toes for twelve hours with only minor blisters. I now wear steel-toes for twelve hours at a time, working outside in the Florida sun, day after day, without a single blister. Actually, more recently, I spent twenty-one hours welding in the Florida heat. This is an all-time record for me.

Steel-toes created the toughness my skin needed so that I could pursue other activities, and now I can buy any pair of shoes or sneakers without worrying about blisters. Steel-toed shoes and boots have pushed my skin to a higher threshold. Be prepared to go through socks, as they tend to rub against your toenails, which eat through the socks. Steel-toes are very painful to wear if you've never worn them. And your feet do not breathe well in them. The doctors will tell you they are unhealthy, and they are correct. I use them as a training mechanism to make my feet tougher. They do make steel-toed clogs as well. I have yet to try them. But if you think buying a cushy pair of shoes is wise, think again. Just as weight lifters must increase their weights to become stronger, people with EB must use harder sneakers and insoles with thinner socks to raise their pain threshold and increase skin toughness. This is a difficult shift to make at first, but it's very beneficial in the long term. You can do this over time: wear the new sneakers or boots for just five or ten minutes a day and work your way up.

As a blue-collar worker, I spend a good deal of time on my knees, making repairs or welding. I found a pair of pants that have helped to reduce and prevent pain and blisters on my knees. They are 5.11 Tactical pants. These are law enforcement and military pants typically called BDUs (battle dress uniforms). They have pockets on the knees that you can slide kneepads into. They are a very comfortable addition to my work gear. They offer outstanding performance on diamond plate floors, which used to really do a number on my knees. I use them when performing home repairs or gardening. My knees are no longer sore or blistered after working for extended periods of time. Knees, unlike feet, require cushioning. For whatever reason, the harder I worked my knees without pads, the more it hurt them and me. There are other manufacturers that offer similar pants. I have yet to experiment with them.

By the way, I look forward to filling out job applications that ask if I have any disabilities or special needs to satisfactorily perform all the tasks. My answer is always the same: no. And I have never needed any. Nobody would know that I have EB if I didn't tell them.

SUMMARY

- Don't buy sneakers or shoes that feel like pillows. Those are good for around the house but not for everyday wear. Also socks should be thin and very breathable.
- Work on conditioning your feet every day. Ask yourself what you can do today that will toughen your skin, and then do it, even if it is for just five minutes. Make a habit of this. Challenge yourself; you might be surprised by the results.
- Try buying steel-toes to toughen your feet. Your skin is like a muscle and needs to be worked.
- Keep the vision of being blister-free. Close your eyes and see and feel what it's like. It works, and it makes you feel great.
- Don't be afraid to try new places, such as a moderate walking trail instead of the easy trail, and different things, maybe a new hobby.
- Patience and persistence pays off.
- Take the job you want even if you think it's not a good choice for your EB. If it doesn't work out, at least you can say you made your best attempt.
- Products, search for, buy and try more products.

CHAPTER 3

The Mind and Attitude

Whatever the mind can conceive and believe,
it can achieve.

—Napoleon Hill

EB was handed down to me from my mother's side of the family—as was all the backward logic, incorrect programming, and really bad advice. It is not their fault, as they were programmed with garbage too. Garbage in, garbage out.

I was programmed to believe that EB is something I just have to live with. Initially I bought into that mindset. My family's idea of prevention and inactivation was to sit on the couch and watch TV. I taught prevention and inactivation to myself. I spent a decade erasing all the incorrect programming that was jammed into my brain. I have been on a very long journey, trying out different products, practices, and attitudes. I have pushed my body and mind to achieve extraordinary things. I have accomplished so many things that a lot of people without EB haven't achieved or attempted.

This thing called EB does not define who we are or what we can do. Once you accept that it exists and that there are ways to live, work, and play around it—or even completely inactivate it as I have with my protocol—then you take matters into your own hands. When you let go of the victim attitude, amazing things begin to happen. Stop telling yourself you have this and start telling yourself that you can be blister-free at all times. Start telling yourself that you can do anything that anyone else can do and start doing those things. Don't stop, ever. You can and will **Eventually Build** your dream life. It will take time to work your way up the ladder, going at your own pace. But you need to push yourself physically each and every time you can.

As an example, say you are typically capable of doing ten to twenty minutes of heavy activity before your skin blisters, and then you take the next two days off. Instead, go for a walk the very next day, even if it's just to the end of the driveway and back. Keep increasing the length of your activity and pushing yourself on the recovery days. I followed an active recovery program during the tough years. It doesn't take a long time or much effort to start seeing results. Your mind will direct your body to overcome and adapt. Consider your skin as a muscle. Work it! I work mine very, very hard—harder than most people without EB. The human body is amazing, and the mind drives it. **Exercise Beyond** what you are capable of, as often as possible, and the skin will adapt.

To this day all my family members still suffer from EB. They take on the mindset that it is something they have and must live with. My uncle Paul has the correct mindset; now he just needs to implement the nutrition plan that is best for him and some other items from my protocol. My other relatives take no preventative measures (unless it's sitting down or forgoing something they wish they could do) and won't try products that may make a difference. But it's more than that: it's an attitude. They would rather undergo treatment than focus on prevention. My mom continues to believe that she and my brother just have it worse than me. This is horseshit. I just took measures throughout my life, reprogrammed my subconscious mind by telling myself I don't have this thing called EB, and continued to try new products that led to greater success. If I stop following the protocol, I get the same results they do. I suffer. This proves to me that my protocol works.

I eat and think differently than my relatives, which is another reason for my success. My EB was just as bad as theirs—so bad, at times, that I couldn't do what I wanted to do. I got made fun of as a kid. I am glad these things happened, as they pushed me to where I am today. I wanted to ride my bike, run, hike, and do everything that all the other kids were doing. But I couldn't. It was embarrassing and painful. At best, I could go for an hour performing any given activity such as street hockey, bike riding, walking, canoeing, etc.. on a hot summer day in New England. Then it was days of recovery.

I felt like it was punishment for living. It was the same for almost all my family members that have EB. We'd have to go back to our rooms, break out the blister pad, and pop all our blisters with a sterilized needle. Then the pain really hit. For some reason, it hurts more to walk on a popped blister than a full one. We'd put socks on if possible and limp away, sometimes unable to put our shoes back on. Some days were so bad that I'd crawl around the house, and then my knees would blister up.

Of all the things in my protocol that were difficult to accept and adapt to, the hardest for me was to overcome the mind and my negative thoughts. When I say "the mind," I'm referring to the subconscious mind. Deep within it live paradigms that control everything you do and the results you get in any given area of your life. According to The Proctor and Gallagher Institute: Paradigms are mental programs that have almost exclusive control over our habitual behavior—and almost all our behavior is habitual. These paradigms are passed down from one family member to the next. Starting your child off with a positive mindset ("You are getting blisters now only because you haven't implemented all the necessary steps or products.") will go a long way toward creating a very positive daily attitude and shaping the child's development. You have until they are approximately seven years old to mold them like a piece of clay, according to healthline.com. The earlier you start telling your child positive things about prevention and inactivation instead of treatment, the faster everyone's life will get better. The mind is the most powerful weapon in your arsenal. Use it wisely and reap the rewards!

It is difficult to see your body riddled with blisters and tell yourself you don't have EB or that you are blister-free. There are a lot of books, courses, and videos out there on the subject of visioneering. It would be very beneficial to start studying them. Tell yourself that you don't have this. Write it out, say it out loud, and train your brain to accept the fact that you can live a normal life. Envision it, emotionally feeling what it would be like not to have EB, to participate in life fully. Fake it till you make it.

I got to the point where I believed it. Then I saw it, and now I am living it, so I know you can too. This didn't happen overnight. It was a decade before I started seeing results, and twice as long until I was living the life I had dreamed about. But now I know this process can be sped up. The more emotion and practice you put behind it, the faster the results will come.

Here is a list of thoughts that *must be thrown out* of your vocabulary and mind:

- EB is something I have and must live with.
- I should take this drug; it might help.
- I should put this chemical agent on my foot; it might help.
- I shouldn't do that because of my EB.
- I can't do that because of my EB.
- I'll never be like everyone else.
- I'll never run a marathon.
- This is something I'll always have.
- There is no cure.

- I'll buy the thick, soft socks.
- I'll buy the softest sneakers.
- I'll buy the thick foam-pad insoles because they are soft and squishy.
- I better be careful with my skin because of my EB.
- I better stay in today because it is too hot outside.

To **Eliminate B**ad thoughts, you must control your mind to say the *opposite* of all the items listed above. Anytime one of them comes up, whether in your mind or in conversation with others, replace it with one of these statements, or feel free to make up your own:

- My feet are beautiful, and I can do anything.
- I will hike that mountain on a one-hundred-degree day.
- I will buy the sneakers I want.
- This is something I was given and is a gift.
- I can do anything because I don't have EB and I am EB-free.
- I will walk in Disney World, in Florida, during the summer. I am so grateful that I can inactivate EB.
- I am so happy for the products that let me achieve greatness.

You must exercise your mind like never before! Sometimes it will be the biggest battle of the day. You must be fully committed to these thoughts. Go ahead; your mind won't blister no matter how hard you work it! I say these positive statements many times throughout the day as I walk for blister-free miles. As I say them, I feel gratitude pour through my body. The negative thoughts that were programmed into me took the longest to change. They literally control how you behave, what your attitude is, which products you purchase, what you'll attempt to do on any given day, who you hang out with, which career you choose, and how well you do it—ultimately, your success in all areas of life. The more you learn to think "I will live blister-free and do what I want, when I want, wherever I want," then the faster you will be on the road to success.

You need to get all this into your subconscious mind. This takes time, especially if you were brought up with all the wrong programming that I endured for many years before I conquered it. I have been very persistent and successful, but believe me, I have had many bad days when I let all the naysayers get into my head. And I still hear it from certain family members—so negative. I wish for you to live the unbelievable life you so deserve. I can't explain what it is like to have the choice to live with EB or not, to stand on top of a mountain that took five hours to summit on an eighty-degree day and hike five hours back down with a forty-pound pack on my back, or to ride a bicycle for eight hours on an even hotter day without getting a single blister anywhere on my body. It is the greatest accomplishment, and it is Euphoric Beyond belief.

Memorize these two statements:

Believing is seeing. Once you believe something in your subconscious mind, it will manifest. I learned this from Bob

Proctor at The Proctor and Gallagher Institute and found it to be true.

You get what you believe, not what you want. This one is very powerful for me. And I found it to be very true. It helps me bust through bad paradigms. All the greats that teach The Law of Attraction preach this. Bob Proctor, Tony Robbins, Wayne Dyer, to name a few.

There are some mind games I played with myself when I was younger, with much success. These games get me to direct my focus on something I want versus what is present, such as a negative thought or feeling. When you are in emotional or physical pain from anything, including blisters, focus on where it doesn't hurt. This lessens or eliminates the pain. If you want to go out and ride a bike but can't because of blisters, get down and do some push-ups and sit-ups. Start a blister journal to track your progress and document changes to see if everything is working or needs adjustment. I always had backup activities to take care of on blister days. I would clean and lubricate my bicycles and envision myself riding longer and faster than the day before. I would plan out my next ride to be about five miles farther (that makes for a round trip of ten extra miles). I just kept stretching until the blisters stopped. I would ask myself "How can I ride one hundred miles without any blisters?" The first answer that came to my mind was "Ride 120 miles." So I did. My mind was correct. After I rode 120 miles, got blisters, and recovered, I could ride one hundred miles without a single blister.

My attitude toward EB changed drastically after I took on the project of a lifetime: to Eventually Behave like everyone else while they run, walk, cycle, hike, and do everything under the sun. I set out to try a variety of products and a different attitude with patience and persistence. It paid off big time. Keep in mind that I mention all these products without receiving any compensation, and the companies or people behind them are not connected to me in any way. I have tried a very wide variety of products—too many to list here—and depending on the results, I either toss them or implement them into my routine.

People without EB will never understand what we feel or go through on a day-to-day basis. They might think they do when they get a blister or two after running a marathon, but they will never truly never understand. Even when they see the feet or body parts covered in blisters, they don't know the psychological and spiritual pain, which is worse than the physical pain, by far. The blisters can heal, but the spirit, if not solidly built, will diminish. This leads to problems such as drinking, depression, and drug use.

Focusing on what doesn't hurt or what is great when you can't even walk to the refrigerator can be a difficult thing to do. Not impossible, but difficult. Try to put things in perspective. As I always said to myself, at least I'm not getting shot at on a battlefield. As soon as I think of soldiers—how they must **E**ndure **B**attles, and what they are thinking about while they are surrounded by chaos—my trip to the fridge on my knees seems just fine. This type of thinking developed my attitude until, when I did get blisters, I would laugh at them. I would tell them they are not long for this world, but I am. I just had to develop my attitude into a better state of mind.

You can see how I have fun by putting the initials EB in bold in other phrases throughout this book. It puts a smile on my face when I create an EB phrase and link it to an event. This is another way I have fun with my EB gift.

A good attitude does wonders for overall health and productivity. It can carry you in many ways: pain management, tolerance, and overall well-being. The pain-management center in my brain has changed dramatically over the years. I can block out a great deal of pain and continue to push forward, especially with my hands and feet. Lewis Burwell "Chesty" Puller "was a highly decorated United States Marine Corps lieutenant general. He is one of the most famous and most decorated Marines in the Corps' history, and is the only Marine to be awarded five Navy Crosses for extraordinary heroism. Puller served in World War I, World War II, and the Korean War. He is also one of only two Marines to be awarded both the Army and Navy Distinguished Service Crosses, according to Britannica." He has a great quote on allgreatquotes.com: "Pain is weakness leaving the body."

Long after I created this protocol, I discovered a book called *Think and Grow Rich* by Napoleon Hill. After reading about how Napoleon Hill's son Blair, who was born without ears, cured his deafness by following the practices that Hill mentions in his book, I realized that I had been using this method to inactivate EB in my body all along and didn't know it.

The story of Hill's son is amazing. He was born in 1912, completely deaf in both ears. Almost two decades later, with the assistance of a device, he could hear, when doctors said he never would. I highly recommended that you buy this book and read it. Do exactly what Hill did with his son's deafness with your EB and watch what happens. Apply these rules to every area of your life. The mind is so powerful. Use it to your advantage and don't let it tell you that you have to live with something you don't want. It takes practice and the use of your higher faculties: will, intuition, perception, memory, imagination, and reason. These will guide you to all the answers you need. The Proctor Gallagher Institute goes into depth about these higher faculties. We all have them and can develop them to higher levels with practice. I am almost certain that you will discover things that I have not.

Another must-read is Maxwell Maltz's *Psycho-Cybernetics*. This book is about how your self-image controls your behavior. Once you elevate your self-image, great things begin to happen. And I bet anyone with EB has suffered from poor self-image from time to time, if not all the time. If you do, or you know someone that does, do yourself a favor and read this book. The books I recommend are classics that have sold millions of copies for many reasons. They provide exercises to help you work out your shortcomings and correct the beliefs or thoughts that hold you back. They also have more amazing stories that you will enjoy from people that have suffered from ailments or diseases.

Now, there are a few people out there who are really good at explaining how to reprogram your subconscious mind and guiding you through the process. From the Proctor Gallagher Institute, Bob Proctor, who recently passed, is the best person I have found for this. Sandy Gallagher, his partner and the

CEO of the company, is also an outstanding resource on the ins and outs of shifting paradigms. The more I follow their guidance the more I learn and speed up my results. I'm just beginning to use this in other areas of my life. As Proctor would be the first to tell you, and I agree, you have your work cut out for you if you don't reprogram your mind. Buy his books, join his programs, or go to one of Proctor Gallagher Institutes seminars. They offer many free courses online. They are masters of how to reprogram your subconscious mind and eliminate bad paradigms. Proctor and his partner Gallagher have a good deal of information on YouTube as well.

Becoming Supernatural: How Common People Are Doing the Uncommon by Dr. Joe Dispenza is a fascinating, very true story. I have yet to master his techniques, but the story of his spinal cord recovery after a bicycle accident is nothing short of a miracle. And his mind controlled the repairs. This book is filled with unbelievable stories of recovery using mind-control techniques to overcome personal battles. Truly inspiring.

Thresholds of the Mind by Bill Harris was the first book about the mind that I read. I need to read this again. I am also a fifteen-year-long student of the Centerpointe Research Institute's Holosync meditation program. I meditate for at least one hour per day (two if time permits) to reduce stress and gain clarity. It really calms my mind. If your mind is going like someone is holding down the change-channel button on the clicker for the TV, then you are a great candidate for meditation. If you have depression, anger, stress, or negative thoughts, or you just want to feel better overall, give it a shot. It is a long-term game, but the benefits speak for themselves.

Richard L. Haight's *The Warrior's Meditation: The Best-Kept Secret in Self-Improvement, Cognitive Enhancement, and Stress Relief, Taught by a Master of Four Samurai Arts* is also a surprisingly great read about the mind, self-improvement, and cognitive enhancement. Haight guides you through the several steps you need to practice to become proficient at the "Warriors Meditation." This is meditating on the fly as a ninja warrior would do. It brings calmness during your busy, hectic day. The surprising parts of this book are that he dives into food allergies, emotions, sleep, fasting, menopause, and much more. You will walk away with a good deal of new information.

But the book that kicked it all off for me was *The Mindbody Prescription: Healing the Body, Healing the Pain* by John E. Sarno, MD. A friend recommended it to me because of my allergies. From this book, I found out that my allergies are created by my mind due to stress. Allergies are trying to take my mind off what is really stressing me out. Stress triggers a fight-or-flight mechanism. There's a lot to think about while reading this one—I learned so much about myself and my thought process.

John Assaraf's *Innercise: The New Science to Unlock Your Brain's Hidden Power* will teach you methods of training your brain and realizing your goals. It's a great read, and I'm still doing his "innercises" today.

- Start reading books on the subconscious mind and paradigm shifts.
- Establish a period of time, preferably in the morning before your day starts, to write down ten things you're grateful for. Include being grateful for your skin, feet, and hands during this exercise.
- Develop and implement daily practices in mind control.
- Give meditation or yoga a try. They are great mind-body tools.
- Find a mentor in the area of mind control and follow them. Do what they say; become a student.

CHAPTER 4

Food and Hydration

Let thy food be thy medicine.

—Hippocrates

Nutrition is right up there next to mind control in importance. It is so important to find a healthy diet that works for you. Everyone and every body is so different that I will not tell you what to do in this category other than to experiment greatly. I will also explain what food lifestyles I choose and the products that I have tried. The difference in performance and recovery is undeniable.

For me, lots of fresh, healthy organic vegetables work best. My skin, body, mind, and muscles love them the most, and I sleep soundly on a healthy diet, which is very important for recovery. I wish I did more with food as a child. But unfortunately I was just eating what was put in front of me.

I try to eat as many cruciferous vegetables as possible every day: broccoli, brussels sprouts, some lettuces (such as arugula and bok choy) and cauliflower. I have found that growing my own non-GMO vegetable garden is the best. I can see and feel results the next day after eating a good, healthy meal. If I am not eating garden-fresh vegetables, I take a product called Phytomax. This is an all-natural, concentrated vegetable pill sold by Hammer Nutrition. I sleep better, my skin looks five years younger, and I have more energy—the list goes on. What a product! I also take Hammer Nutrition's daily vitamins, and their products are derived from natural ingredients. I consider taking them to be a very important part of my daily routine. I view them as a must-have for anyone over the age of thirty. Our bodies just don't do what they used to without assistance, and I have learned that I can reverse the clock, so to speak, by implementing all these dietary choices and taking these supplements.

I do eat free-range, grass-fed organic proteins. I also eat vegan proteins. A company called Gardein makes some really good plant-based foods. But I avoid the products they sell with wheat in them. I try and stay clear of bread, bread crumbs, breaded or battered fried foods, anything with wheat or gluten in it. According to hopkinsmedicine.org, wheat and gluten are not something that the body was designed to digest and break down. It contributes to a lot of my skin issues: rashes, blisters, acne, and itching. After 30 years of suffering with chronic shoulder pain, severe throat clearing and discolored nails, I discovered mushrooms to be the cause. I love mushrooms but can no longer eat them. The pros of eliminating them from my diet far outweigh the cons. I have also become very proficient at reading the ingredients list the first time I put any food product into my shopping carriage. I spend time at the store, researching the ingredients listed on the package and what purpose they have. You would be surprised by what manufacturers will put in your food. The day after getting severe acne on my face, I found out that I had eaten jet-fuel stabilizer for dinner. It was listed in the ingredients as BHT, according to Wikipedia, it is used in the petroleum industry as AO-29, used in jet fuels, hydraulic fluids and gear oils. Why is it being added into my food? And the FDA (Food and Drug Administration) approves this for use in our food!

Yes, you read that correctly: jet-fuel stabilizer. It was on the label as BHT (butylated hydroxytoluene); look that one up. I hadn't taken the time to read the label because it said it was organic and non-GMO. Yet when I called to question the company about this, I received no answer. You must be vigilant with this. Garbage in, garbage out.

At a health seminar, I learned about a product called Udo's Oil 3-6-9 Blend. It was invented by a man named Udo Erasmus which you can learn all about his fascinating journey on the development of this product at www.udoerasmus. com. Please take the time to do your research on this product, which has had an enormously positive effect on my skin, digestion, and performance. Udo's Oil 3-6-9 Blend is an organic omega-3, -6, and -9 fatty acid oil derived from flax-, sesame-, and sunflower-seed oils. Our bodies do not make these fatty acids, which are an important component of your cell membranes. About a week of taking this oil has resulted in the significant reduction of my mild eczema issues (related to my hyperkeratosis), the elimination of dryness and heavy cracking in my heels (also due to hyperkeratosis), a significant reduction in acne, healthier-looking skin overall, more strength and energy, and faster recovery times from exercise and injuries, just to name a few improvements. You may not like the taste, but you'll love the benefits. I drink it either straight up, with my meals, or oddly enough, in my coffee, where it tastes awesome. I drink my coffee black, as sugar and cream are not good on a daily basis.

I had the distinct pleasure of meeting and speaking with Udo one-on-one at a seminar, and we had a great conversation about oils. I learned so much, especially about cooking with oils. Don't do it! Do your research on this and stop cooking or frying with oil; I learned from Udo during my one on one with him that it is not the healthy option and he can explain why. Butter is better. I just love what educating yourself can do. His website goes into details about all of this and he's very open and would love to hear from you with any questions you may have.

Fasting plays a very important role in my health and recovery. My body loves intermittent fasting. Do your research and experiment with this practice, www.jennycraig.com has some information on this. Intermittent fasting has had an amazing effect on my skin and overall well-being.

Juicing is an area that you should try or, at the very least, research. I love a glass of freshly squeezed orange juice in the morning. I play around with various juices, and they have a significant impact on my skin, bowel movements, sleep, the maintenance of a healthy weight, the elimination of inflammation, detox, and so on. I first learned about juicing from Charlotte Gerson and Morton Walker's *The Gerson Therapy: The Proven Nutritional Program to Fight Cancer and Other Illnesses*. 2001. You'll be amazed by what proper nutrition can do for your mind, body and soul.

Hydration is super important for people with EB. Make sure you're getting enough water. Proper hydration is very important. It seems counterintuitive, but the more water I drink, the more I can push my body. I drink bottled water, and I make sure it says 100 percent spring water in the ingredients. You wouldn't believe what they are putting in spring water. Scary stuff. Tap water is no good in most areas. As a licensed water and waste water treatment specialist I was performing water testing every day on a variety of residential, municipal and industrial water systems. According to the Center for Disease Control and Prevention, municipal waterworks typically put chlorine in the water to kill bacteria. Then they add ammonia to give the chlorine staying power while it travels through miles of pipes. This mixture creates chloramines—which are not good to put in the body, according to springwellwater.com, although the EPA states that they're safe. So now you have chloramines and jet fuel stabilizer in your system! How do you expect your body to function with these in your system? You can find extensive information about all the items listed above on the world wide web. You can also visit www.epa.gov and educate yourself in this matter. I bet everyone working at the EPA is drinking bottled water as well. Tap water with chloramines is great for doing dishes, laundry, or washing vehicles. Well water is typically good to drink, but you'll need to get a water analysis done to see what is coming out of your tap. You can educate yourself on well water at a variety of websites. Or go to www.culligan.com to learn more about water and water filtration.

It's logical that blisters more easily develop from dry, irritated skin. If you are hydrating properly, then this keeps your skin moist and supple. Keep in mind that you need to dial in the correct amount of water for your body, your activity levels, and the temperature outside. This took some time for me to do, as will everything you are experimenting with in the implementation phase. I start off slowly and work my way up or down, depending on the results. There can also be long lag times between the implementation phase and the results phase. I usually stick to a month or two whenever I try a new product, practice, food, or level of water intake. This gives my body time to flush out the old and take in the new, and time for me to recognize results. However, you may need only a few weeks. But experimentation is key.

Foods I avoid include sugar, wheat, gluten, alcohol on a regular basis (especially beer, which has wheat in it), anything with preservatives in it, and breaded or battered fried foods

Drugs I avoid include anything made in a laboratory. This includes antibiotics; which in my opinion are not good for your internal systems. I don't believe in any of them. However, I understand the need for them. I was mountain biking in the Tyrolean Alps once, and I fell off my bike and landed in fine gravel covered in duck shit. I rushed home and showered like crazy, trying to get it all out of the road rash on my arm. Twenty-four hours later, I could see and feel a red line crawling up my arm, heading toward my heart and head. I went to the hospital to get checked out and sure enough, infection had started. They put me on antibiotics. These things happen, and that's what they are there for. I'm not in the habit of taking them just in case or at the first sign of a red halo around a blister. But I do monitor the situation closely, and if needed, I know where the hospital is. If I eat, sleep, and think correctly, my body runs like a charm with no infections. I have not had a blister infection in at least twenty years, maybe thirty. The same goes for pain medications. I don't believe in taking something to hide something. How will I become stronger?

If you must take antibiotics for a problem, counter them with probiotics. I have a probiotic product daily (one in the morning and one in the evening). Increased energy levels, regular bowel movements, and the significant or total elimination of flatulence all day are but a few benefits of this regimen. Gut health is critical to overall well-being and proper functioning.

Here is a list of diets or food programs that I have experimented with. I have some portion of each in my daily food regimen:

- *The JJ Virgin Diet: Drop 7 Foods; Lose 7 Pounds, Just 7 Days*, by fitness expert JJ Virgin. This diet identifies and corrects food intolerances. I learned about my food allergies with her program. Mine are wheat, corn, and store-bought eggs. When I eliminated these items from my daily intake for thirty days, all kinds of strange issues disappear: unbearable shoulder pain, acne, bowel issues, and joint pains that seemed to pop up randomly.

- *The Engine 2 Diet: The Texas Firefighter's 28-Day Save-Your-Life Plan that Lowers Cholesterol and Burns Away the Pounds* by Rip Esselstyn. This is a plant-based program that helps you live a healthier lifestyle. Engine 2 products can be found in grocery stores and are really tasty and healthy. Give them a shot.

- The Snake Diet was developed by Cole Robinson. His YouTube videos are funny, entertaining, and informative. I had good luck with this program. The name stems from how wildlife tends to eat, then have periods of fasting while drinking just water with some salt. It is a detox system.

- The Gerson Therapy developed by Dr. Max Gerson—I experimented with this early on and had great luck with it. Gerson has many documented cases of curing all kinds of diseases, including cancers. His secretary made an attempted assassination on him to stop his practice and eventually forced his family practice out of the country. This you can read about online or in the book The Killing of a Cure. The Murder of Max Gerson.

- Vegan and raw vegan are some of my favorite ways to eat.

- I eat a vegetarian diet with salads as often
  as possible.

SUMMARY

- Develop a nutrition plan that your body loves and
  stick with it.
- Experiment greatly to find what works and
  what doesn't.
- Be aware of lag times—some, if not all, dietary
  changes can take a month to produce results.
- Eat cruciferous vegetables daily.
- Get to know your food intolerances. Certain foods
  affect your body tremendously and can cause all
  kinds of health issues. www.advancedbodyscan.com.
- Try to avoid drugs of any kind. Our bodies were
  not made to run on them. I'm talking about pain-
  killers or other unnecessary pills for easing life's
  daily stressors.

CHAPTER 5

Footwear and Clothing

I firmly believe that with the right footwear one can rule the world.

—Bette Midler

I bet I would have a million extra dollars if it weren't for what I have spent on sneakers, shoes, underwear, boots, sandals, socks, creams, and oils, and I continue to purchase and experiment with products, trying to build a better mousetrap. I recently tried Allbirds sneakers and Giesswein hiking boots, two different companies. They piqued my interest because of the materials they are made from. Materials matter to people with EB more than they do to the general population. These products, both Allbirds and Giesswein, are made from wool, and I had never worn a wool shoe or boot. Unfortunately they were too narrow for my feet, and I had to return both pairs. They do not manufacture larger widths at this time.

But I have discovered a sock that is worthy of mention. It's from the Darn Tough Vermont sock company. The socks are made out of merino wool and provide excellent fit and function. These socks are not cheap, but right out of the gate, I noticed a total or almost total reduction in foot odor, depending on what I'm doing that day. If I do have odor, then it's at a level I can tolerate without wearing a clothespin on my nose. They are more comfortable than traditional cotton socks, and they feel great on my feet. The stitching, which my feet do not notice, is really precise and fine.

Darn Tough Vermont also describes the socks as antimicrobial, which is an added must-have for folks with EB. My feet absolutely love these socks. They have had a tremendous impact on my foot comfort and foot health. After three weeks of wearing Darn Tough Vermont socks, my yellow and discolored toenails showed signs of clearing up, the fungus under them dried up, and I had much happier, cleaner-smelling feet. I think I have already spent close to $500 on them, and I have donated all my old socks to charity. The company offers so many weights, heights, styles, and colors. I initially bought two pairs. The positive results were drastic enough that, after less than a week of wearing them, I went back online and spent over a hundred dollars to get more. My favorites are the tactical socks and the lightweight lifestyle socks. These are two different styles of socks that the company offers. The heavyweight socks are great for living in colder areas. I needed the next size up in sneakers and boots to accommodate them, but they're highly effective nonetheless. The socks are another win for my feet! Buy one pair and you'll never wear another sock. They are guaranteed for life and hold up really well in steel-toed boots. My big toenail wears a hole through standard cotton socks but not these. I tried Kevlar-toed socks in the past for this issue, but my feet did not agree with them.

After six to eight months of blister-free living, I discovered a new pair of socks from Allbirds. They are made from trees, though I'm not sure what kind—part of the process is experimentation. So I purchased a pair and wore them for a long day at work. My boss yelled at me and accused me of not doing my job, so I let myself become stressed; my self-esteem lowered, and I became angry. I came home from work after a twelve-hour day in these socks, poured a shoulder dropper (my term for a shot of bourbon), and down the hatch it went.

About an hour later, I felt three blisters developing on my left foot. I took the socks off after wearing them for about fourteen hours and saw the key indicator of blisters forming: bright red marks. Twenty years ago, my feet and hands would have been riddled with full-blown blisters under these conditions. To eliminate stress and alcohol from the equation, which can promote blister formation, I will try these socks again down the road, on a hike or a long walk. Then I will know if these socks work for me or not. I need to note here that red wine gives me more blisters than bourbon. And beer is the most blister-promoting drink for me.

I can say this about Allbirds socks after wearing them for a long day: no foot odor. But to be 100 percent positive before buying many pairs, I will retest them once my foot has recovered. The three blisters I have on my left foot in no way affect my walking, running, or hiking capabilities, as they are small and in areas of the foot that I can hardly feel. This is what I mean by a significant reduction in blisters. I do tend to get blisters, small in number and size, when I'm trying different products. I get excited when I do blister—I can eliminate the product or practice!

If you are like I used to be, then you get blisters all around your crotch as well. I switched to Under Armour underwear. All gone, 100 percent, and no crotch rot! Under Armour is made from materials that breath well and doesn't retain sweat and bacteria. You can go to the website and read about the materials used in their products. Remember this as you read the ingredients and materials list on any products you buy. Try to eliminate cotton products that come into direct contact with your skin. Cotton retains moisture and odor. In addition, open blisters and wounds stick to cotton more easily. This can really do damage when the remaining skin or scab is ripped off. There is a whole world of other materials out there that your body will fall in love with and thank you for.

Even thirty years after starting my protocol, I'm improving it by adding and deleting products. My mindset is the same, focusing on what I desire versus what is present, only now, it's permanent and easy. I don't even think about blisters.

I remember when trying on all the sneakers in the store, looking for the right pair, was an all-day affair. I'd pray that the first pair felt best to reduce my shopping time, but no such luck. Most of the time, I would have to drive to multiple stores, only to repeat the process all over again. All day, sometimes all weekend, to buy one pair of sneakers! If people without EB knew just half of what we do, they'd have a better understanding of what it's like to live with it. What an Enormous Backache that used to be. Now it is a very quick, typically once-a-year process for me. I actually get excited to do it now, and when I find something I like, I usually buy two or three pairs. Sneakers are always getting discontinued, so when I buy the right pair, I buy a lot of the right pair. That way, I don't have to come back, and I have reliable backups.

I exclusively wear New Balance sneakers and trail runners. For steel-toed, low-top, and over-the-ankle boots, I prefer the Timberland PRO series. The materials that manufacturers use in their products matter to our overall foot health. I will walk out of a store with three different pairs of the same sneakers so that I not only don't have to deal with another all-day affair of shoe shopping for a long time, but also I have shoes that I really like and make my feet happy in the event that they're discontinued. The sneakers I'm wearing now are the New Balance 410v6 cross-trainer. It feels like I have air-conditioning for my feet. But, by far, my absolute favorite and most comfortable New Balance is the 993. It is a running sneaker but my feet absolutely love this sneaker. Get ready to shell out about $200.00. They are American made.

By playing with sizing and widths over the years, I have determined that extra wide and half a size up are what my feet love most. I believe that proper fit is critical to foot comfort and blister reduction. My feet particularly do not like standard sneakers, and that is what I wore in my early years.

My feet love sandals, and the brand does not seem to matter. No matter what I wear, sandals don't seem to cause any pain, soreness, or blisters. Some are better than others for walking long distances. I'm currently wearing SAS, San Antonio Shoe sandals and they are a nice sandal to wear. A little to soft for me but they are good for around the house or short walks. I also really liked Sperry Top-Siders. My feet loved them as well. I bought a pair in Bar Harbor, Maine, and they instantly fit like a glove. I should have purchased three pairs as they have since discontinued this style product.

Do you get blisters around the waistline from wearing belts? I did. Then I found that moisturizing around the waist five or ten minutes before putting on any clothing, letting the oil or lotion work its way in, reduces or eliminates this. I wear lined duty belts from DeSantis. The lining adds an extra strip of material on the inside of the belt that reduces discomfort after long periods of wearing belts. They are very comfortable and create little to no pressure points, as I had experienced with other brands. I also buy belts of different widths so I can rotate them daily, giving the skin I worked yesterday a break. Their cost ranges greatly depending on their style, length, and width. I have had mine for about twenty years. They still look new and haven't stretched much.

I carry a firearm, which my skin took some time to get used to. I find that alternating holsters, holster styles, and carry locations work well for me. I carry blister-free now.

Looking back, I saw small measures of improvement with some of the products that I tried, while others provided instant, very noticeable improvements. I love large, quick gains when I try a new product. It does amazing things for your self-confidence when you can go a little further, a little longer, with a smile, knowing you're on the road to greatness!

SUMMARY

- Buy a pair of Darn Tough Vermont socks today, without hesitation, and put them to the test.
- Give New Balance sneakers a shot. I have had the best luck with their American-made sneakers.
- Always work on your self-confidence and self-image; these matter.
- Always bring your orthotics when shopping for shoes. Put them in the shoes that you're trying on.
- Wear the socks you wear daily on your shoe-shopping trips.
- Switch sneakers and socks often on hot, sweaty days. Wet, soggy feet are a buzzkill and create blisters.
- Stop wearing cotton on your hands, feet and crotch.

CHAPTER 6

Foot Odor and Stress

*It is not a daily increase but a daily decrease.
Hack away at the inessentials.*

—Bruce Lee

One thing that used to bother me the most about my EB was the odor of my feet. More often than not, on a scale of one (not so smelly) to ten, very stinky (wife tells you to get out of the house or she'll leave), I'd fall in the six or seven zone. What's funny is that if I ask my brother how bad his feet smell, he'll say he falls into the same zones, but I bet if we ask our wives, they'd put us at ten plus.

Here is what I'm learning: for anyone that has smelly feet, even people without EB, buy Darn Tough Vermont socks. As

I mentioned, there is a whole world of materials out there to improve your life and foot happiness.

One day while working at my desk, under a lot of stress and stretched thin, I noticed that I had underarm odor—more than usual. I had applied deodorant in the morning. When I got home, my feet smelled like a ten or more. Really bad. Yet without stress, I can work out in a field all day during the summer without any deodorant and come in smelling fine. I began to pay more attention to the stress in my life and how it can create more odor and sweat. I can't explain why stress created an overabundance of foul smell. A few people at the office, both male and female, have stated the same thing: that they, too, notice that they have more odor under stress. I have implemented meditation, exercise, and yoga, all in an effort to reduce or eliminate stress. According to Bob Proctor, stress and depression, it's something we do to ourselves, not something we have. It comes from a concentrated focus on what you don't want. This falls into the mind category, and we need to continuously build our minds to let stress and depression fall by the wayside. Try this to eliminate stress, anxiety and depression: The Wim Hof Method. www.wimhofmethod.com. I get amazing results from following his free breathing method on you tube. Any way you can eliminate or reduce stress is healthy and beneficial, for a multitude of reasons far beyond foot odor. Make a journal or take mental notes about when you are stressed and see if it affects your odor. For me, no stress plus correct footwear plus proper nutrition equals odor-free feet.

I do have an issue with deodorants. For some reason, they all make my underarms irritated and cause blisters, especially toward the end of the stick. I can get away with applying deodorant every other day. I don't know most of the ingredients on the label, but none of them are good for you or your skin, in my opinion. I'm sure it is one of the ingredients I'm unable to pronounce that is causing the irritation and blisters. I have tried all the natural deodorants, but they delivered marginal results at best. I am always searching for alternatives. When the blisters are the thin, clear type that pops very easily with my fingers rather than a needle and don't come that often or hurt, I really don't spend too much time thinking about them. They also do not affect my performance or attitude at all. I will eliminate deodorants of this type eventually. The chemicals listed on the label do not belong on a human body in my opinion, especially for us EB folks. And following my protocol, I do not blister using deodorants.

Hyperkeratosis is the leading cause of my foot odor. Hyperkeratosis is a condition marked by the thickening of the outer layer of skin, which is made of keratin, a tough protective protein that can cause calluses, eczema, and other disorders. These issues can come from aggressive soaps, nutritional deficiencies (vitamin A), or side effects from drugs. I thought for sure that my toes were the problem but upon smelling my socks after removal, I realized that the majority of the odor came from my heels. Stinky socks will not lie to you. When I stay on top of the hyperkeratosis, I stay on top of the odor. I feel great, have less pain, and have beautiful, functioning feet. I spend about half an hour a week keeping hyperkeratosis at bay. In the beginning, it was out of control and took about two hours a week. It was painful work to get rid of it, but I am glad I figured out a way to do it. It was really heavy on my feet. I don't wish it on anyone.

SUMMARY

- Determine which area your foot odor is coming from. Then develop ways to address it.
- Be aware of odor levels. It is a key indicator of foot and body performance and health, along with stress levels.
- Incorporate ways to reduce or eliminate stress through meditation, yoga, outdoor activities or whatever makes you happy and takes your mind off of what's bothering you.

CHAPTER 7

Foot Maintenance

Take care of your body. It's the only place you have to live.

—Jim Rohn

Two or three times per week, I perform what I call foot maintenance. I can skip one maintenance day, but not two. It is now a part of my hygiene routine, like brushing my teeth, flossing, changing the bedsheets, and so on. I do a visual inspection of the nails to see if they need to be filed and trimmed. After every shower, I wipe my feet completely dry with a towel and let them air out for a couple of minutes before I put on socks. In addition to having EB growing up, I was born with my metatarsals growing downward instead of straight out. The metatarsals connect your ankle to your toes. They help provide balance when you stand and walk. I was also born with very high arches, which triples the excitement! See, I was born with three gifts! The high arches create direct pressure points on the balls of my feet, which leads to large calluses forming after about two weeks of activity. I must manage them on a regular basis. If I don't, they create foot pain and whole-body fatigue.

As I mentioned earlier, I suffered significantly from hyperkeratosis, which people with EB tend to get. Mine is so bad that large crevices open up on my heels and begin to bleed. Then I favor other areas of my feet when I walk, which exhausts them and creates more pain, up to the point that I am unable to walk without significant pain, which can be unbearable. But I am able to tiptoe around.

I attacked this problem with such tenacity. I use an item you can buy at CVS or Walgreens called Onyx Professional's Foot Rasp and pumice stone. I paid about nine dollars for it, and it works fantastic at keeping my hyperkeratosis in check. I must use it a minimum of two times per week to stay on top of my hyperkeratosis—more often during the winter months, for some reason. I suffer from hyperkeratosis far less, if at all, during the summer and now that I live in Florida, but it took several months to get it under control. In the past I used a surgical blade to remove the heavy portions of hyperkeratosis on my heels and the calluses created by my metatarsals, then smoothed them all out with pumice stones. Hyperkeratosis is the largest contributor to my foot odor. To remove it, I start with the most aggressive tool, the Onyx rasp, which actually looks like a cheese grater, it's aggressive at removal, then work my way to the fine pumice stones to smoothen it all out. I do this while in the hot shower to soften up the outer layer of skin, and it makes a big difference in how quickly I can reduce the build-up when the hyperkeratosis becomes soft.

I am down to using the Onyx and fine pumice stone, two to three times a week to keep it in check. And it doesn't take long: about five minutes per foot in the shower. Early on, I took off too much too fast. That led to very tender feet. I had to learn to gradually take off a little at a time. My toenails used to be almost three-eighths of an inch thick, black, brittle, and ugly. I had to use shop tools to clip my nails. Now I use what everyone else uses: a toenail clipper and a file. I have to trim my nails about every two weeks because there is a point at which my nail length—about one-eighth of an inch—will create blisters on my toes. I have to keep my nails cut close to the skin so there is no length. This took me years to realize. I also spend time cleaning under the nails and, if time permits, taking an Epsom salt bath. I love timing foot maintenance with going to the beach. My feet and skin love saltwater and sand, which are the absolute best for my skin and fungus control and far healthier than a chlorine foot bath or swimming in chlorinated pools, in my opinion.

Whenever possible, I walk barefoot, especially outside. This toughens the skin and is considered grounding or earthing. It is very healthy for your skin to touch dirt and sand. Learn more at www.verywellhealth.com. My feet just love walking on beach sand or a campground road covered in dirt, rocks, and pine needles. It takes a week or two to toughen the skin, but I believe that not wearing socks and sneakers is the best for folks with EB. Start out on small walks and increase as you go. It's all about pushing yourself, raising both your mind's and skin's thresholds. I would love to walk barefoot twenty-four seven. Unfortunately, my trade dictates that I need to wear steel-toes.

You may find this odd, but I touch my feet and give them a massage. I tell my feet that I love them, that I'm grateful for them because they take me everywhere, and that they are beautiful. When I used to be all blistered up, I hated my feet. This was improper thinking that caused more pain. Improper thinking puts you in a bad vibration. Once you're in a bad vibration, bad things begin to unfold. The more I love my feet and the more we do together, the better vibration I fall into. When I'm in a great vibration, more answers and products just seem to fall into my lap to take me to the next level of in-activating EB and keeping it away. All my foot maintenance techniques, which are pretty standard, create better-looking, better-performing, better-smelling feet.

I shower every night before bed and always after long, strenuous exercise. Keeping the feet clean and dry is import-ant. I bring extra socks and underwear with me for quick changes whenever I'm participating in heavy-sweat activities or in the summer months. And I keep an extra pair of very comfortable sneakers in the trunk of my car during the sum-mer and boots during the winter.

I inspect my footwear on a monthly basis. I find that this keeps me from walking on bad footwear and prevents any soreness. I also pull out my insoles and wash them.

SUMMARY

- Develop a foot-maintenance plan that addresses your major issues. Tweak it as you go. It may take some time, but it will be well worth it. Buy the tools needed to do this yourself.
- Determine the best toenail length for your feet and keep them at that length consistently.
- Walk barefoot whenever and wherever possible.
- Tell yourself how much you love your feet and treat them as if you were at a spa getting the royal treatment. Keep them very clean.
- Conduct regular inspections of all footwear that is worn on a daily basis. Replace shoes at the first sign of wear to prevent issues. I use worn shoes for gardening or yard work.

CHAPTER 8

The Protocol

You'll see key words in the title of my book, *Everyday Beliefs*: significantly reduce or inactivate your EB. I'd like to go over inactivation. I have currently inactivated my EB. Simply put, it lays dormant due to my thoughts, how I fuel my body, and so on. I will not get a blister from performing my day-to-day activities or jobs, no matter how hard or long I work my body. If I decide tomorrow to start a new activity, say rock climbing for example, something I've never done before, then I'm sure that I would eventually feel the onset of soreness in the tips of my fingers and toes because I never work those areas of my body like that, which is the first step in blister creation. If I continued climbing, then soreness would shift to redness of the skin. Then would come the blisters. If I practice climbing over a period of a couple of months, then I would develop the skin to tolerate this new activity, and I would not get a blister again, provided I'm following my protocol.

I typically continue until the red mark or the blister. A blister is better for me because then I'm at the beginning of toughening up my skin. The blister I get is equivalent to what someone without EB would experience from the same amount of activity. My EB is inactivated for everything I need it to be, running, walking, welding, and everything that I perform on a day-to-day basis. But not for what is a new activity that creates pressure points or friction in areas of my body that I have not previously conditioned. I could elect to stop climbing at the point of soreness. Sometimes I do, depending on what my schedule looks like or what other activities I have on the agenda. I like to push myself to get blisters in this new area of my body to speed the process up, but I stop at the very beginning of blisters. I do not continue unless I'm forced to. Then I repeat the activity as soon as possible.

This process can be quick or not so quick, depending on the goal at hand and how aggressively I go at it. Remember, I have to develop the muscles for this new activity, and this takes time as well. My muscles and skin are now on the same recovery timer. My skin adapts and becomes tougher much more quickly with this method. I can develop my skin to overpower all my muscles. My muscles will fail after about ten hours of doing the activity at a pretty good level of intensity, and my skin is still blister-free. It's a great feeling when you have inactivated your EB and your skin outperforms your muscles!

My current protocol has been developed over the course of many years—three decades and counting, to be precise. Here is a list of practices and attitudes that I perform daily, weekly, and yearly. The list also includes the products I use. This is the maintenance manual, so to speak, for my body, just like for a car. I follow it for the best performance and health. More importantly, I do it so I can not only walk like everyone else but walk better than everyone else.

The daily protocol—this is what I have to do every day to ensure a blister-free day:

- Change my shoes and socks after work or exercise. I'll wear up to three different pairs of socks, sneakers, underwear or boots in a day, sometimes more depending on weather.
- Use Hammer Nutrition products (Daily Essentials, Phytomax, AO Booster, Tissue Rejuvenator, and others). I follow the recommended doses and have great results that are very noticeable and quick.
- Use Good Feet insoles and orthotics. I have two different pairs of orthotics, one type for everyday walking and another for cycling, skiing, and so on.
- Wear Under Armour underwear.
- Drink lots of water—I stay hydrated (your quantity will be determined by you). I drink enough so that I'm urinating at least one time per hour. Twice an hour is optimal for my body.

- Use moisturizing lotion on my hands and feet, depending on the activity I'm about to engage in. See a list of lotions below.
- Take on the attitude of gratitude.
- Tell myself I can and will.
- Celebrate every day that I have beaten EB.
- Use Udo's Oil 3-6-9 Blend (I follow the recommended serving on the bottle).
- Use Flora Super 8 Hi-Potency Probiotics.
- Wear Darn Tough Vermont socks.
- Increase my activity each and every day that I can.
- Eat lots of organic vegetables and drink freshly squeezed orange juice.
- Take at least one twenty-minute walk per day out in the fresh air.
- Meditate one hour per day using Holosync from the Centerpointe Research Institute.
- Clean and dry my feet well, sometimes twice a day if I am very active.

I can skip some or all these steps for a day or two without noticing much difference. Sometimes on vacations, I do go without them for a week or two, and I may or may not get a couple of small blisters and some soreness. But my recovery is swift.

The weekly protocol:

- Undertake foot maintenance as outlined in Chapter 7.

- Wash the insoles of all my shoes.
- Fast for up to two days (but typically one) in a week. This could mean just skipping one meal per day or skipping them all. I let my body decide. Or as a powerful mind exercise, I'll tell my mind to fast whether my body wants to or not.
- Research and purchase products to experiment with.
- Inspect toenails and trim if needed.
- Remove callus and keratosis buildup found anywhere on my feet twice per week.
- Skip most of my weekly maintenance only during vacations.

The annual protocol:
- Purchase new Good Feet insoles. I purchase six pairs every time. The Good Feet Store will tell me they last a year, and I correct them every time. I get six months out of them if I'm lucky. I am very active, and I wear these and my sneakers and boots out very quickly. Good Feet orthotics are guaranteed for life, and I've never had a problem with them. I had a twenty-year-old pair crack recently while hiking Mount Washington. They exchanged them for new ones, no questions asked.
- Purchase all new footwear. I experiment with cross-trainers, hiking boots, walking and running shoes, and whatever else I see.

- Purchase all new socks. My socks wear thin at the
  heels and toes. So I always send them back to Darn
  Tough Vermont under warranty. They replace them
  free of charge.
- Review my protocol to see if I need to change,
  update, or add anything that I have learned or want
  to try.

I do not skip the yearly steps in the protocol, because I
need the new sneakers, footwear, and socks to keep my feet
happy. Other non-negotiables that I strictly adhere to include:

- Study and work the mind every day.
- Write down ten things I'm grateful for every morning, and I include my skin and feet in the list.
- Use visioneering to see myself successfully complet-
  ing a very hot and strenuous activity blister-free.
- Experiment with products.
- Push my body and mind to do what I want them
  to do.
- Think positively about myself, my situation, and
  my body.
- Don't listen to people who feed me horseshit—this
  applies to family members and spouses as well. I
  find that the people closest to me feed me the most
  harmful information and advice and are capable of
  copious amounts of criticism.

If I skip the bold bullets above, I pay the price. It is not worth it.

Additional steps I take after prolonged activity:

- Remove shoes and socks and let the feet dry out.
- Drink water if I am not already hydrated.
- Take an Epsom salt bath.
- Relax and elevate my feet if I can.
- Jump into the ocean, if possible, and relax on the beach.
- Clean and massage my feet with my hands or put a golf ball on the floor and roll my foot around on it. Massaging the feet is very therapeutic. They will thank you for it.
- Put on fresh socks and sneakers. It's best to put nothing on, but if you must, do not put on the same socks and sneakers worn during an activity.
- Let my feet have time after I've punished them. This is when I take it easy and sit on the couch or a comfy chair with a glass of wine.

I have spent a small fortune on oils, lotions, and creams. The ones I have used or am experimenting with are listed below. I use considerably less lotion now that I use Udo's Oil 3-6-9 Blend. Lotions, depending on what I use, can contribute to foot odor or blisters. I use lotions prior to heavy activities during summer months, as a preventive measure, and after my foot maintenance. I experiment with these all the time. I have yet to find a dedicated, outstanding product that I can buy a case of—a must-have. And I never thought to document the ones I threw away due to issues.

I have found that I can apply lotion just once per day. Applying twice per day leaves me with a very mushy feeling in my socks and lots of extra odor. Not so much foot odor as the socks I wear have taken care of that, but rather the odor of the product is what I'll smell. Even if I apply it before bed, then wake up and apply more before my activity, then that is a bad thing for me. I apply a light coat on my feet and hands in the morning, at the start of the day, and that is it. If I take a midday shower after an activity, I will apply it again. But after my end-of-day shower, just before bed, I do not apply any lotions. I let my feet breathe, so to speak. This is an area that is highly individualized, and you need to spend the money (some products will empty the wallet) and the time to experiment. Lotions were a huge part of my success early on. They seem to be phasing out of my protocol organically as time goes on and I evolve.

I'm currently using Cetaphil, Cracked Skin Repair Lotion once per day, in the morning after I wake up. In the past I've also used Aveeno, coconut oils from various manufacturers, Vermont Premium Emu Oil, and Skintifique Hydrating Gel (made for EB folks). I have aloe vera plants that I break off pieces from, trim and cut to release the gel, then spread gel all over my feet. I started planting these plants all around my property so that in the future, once I have enough of them, I can use them as an everyday product.

As for shaving products, I eliminated shaving cream years ago, partly due to the fact that I couldn't pronounce any of the ingredients on the bottles, and some gave me skin irritation. I shave in a hot shower using nothing but water. It works better than shaving creams, as the steam opens up the pores of the skin and allows the razor to dig deeper, grabbing more hair. It's a very close shave. I start shaving towards the end of my hot shower, so the pores have plenty of time to heat up and open wide. Eliminating shaving cream will also add a few extra bucks to your budget to buy other products listed in this protocol.

I use only the highest-quality Gillette razor blades that I can get my hands on. I prefer the Gillette Fusion but have also used in the past Harry's, Bic, Schick, and others.

As for laundry detergents, I have yet to experiment with them and probably won't, as they don't seem to affect my skin. The same goes for fabric softeners.

SUMMARY

- Develop your own protocol and foot-maintenance program that works for your feet and schedule. Keep it evolving and try new products as they are released.
- Start at once to study the mind and the role it plays in your well-being and blisters.
- Experiment greatly with lotions, as each one has different ingredients and results.
- Let results drive your decisions and product purchases and create your list of non-negotiables.

- Track the successes and failures of the foot-maintenance program that you follow.
- Start your day with an attitude of gratitude and tell
  yourself you love your skin and feet.
- Be patient and understanding toward yourself at all
  times. You are learning to navigate a unique ship.
- Avoid wearing cotton on your hands, crotch and
  feet.

CHAPTER 9

Doing the Impossible

(or What You Thought Was Impossible)

Start doing what's necessary, then what's possible,
and suddenly you are doing the impossible.
—St. Francis of Assisi

I am including a bunch of my personal experiences here to show you what type of life I live following this current protocol. These are the things that I never thought were possible in my younger years. I love celebrating these miracles because it shows me that I can do anything I put my mind to.

Just three or four years ago, my daughter was going to pay me a visit from Austria (she was not born with EB). What an opportunity, I thought, to take her to Disney World—in July. Have you ever been to Florida in July? It's camel's-ass-in-the-desert hot! I applied all my protocol measures leading up to, during, and after this event. I remember certain family members telling me that I couldn't walk Disney for an entire day in the Florida summer because of my feet. How was I going to manage?

I started hydrating the night before and drank plenty of water on the one-hour ride to Disney. I drank no alcohol two nights before or during the day. We were one of the first cars there and began our Disney journey at approximately 8:30 a.m. More than twelve hours and at least a gallon of water later, I was still walking without a single blister anywhere on my feet or body. We did the entire park and rode as many rides as we could, standing in line for forty-five minutes for the more popular ones, and Florida was hot and sunny that day. After the fireworks, which start around 9:00 p.m. and finish around 10:00 p.m., I was still standing on my feet and walking around, blister-free. I remember my aunt saying she got a blister (she does not have EB) and being simply amazed that I did not get one. Certain family members still don't believe me when I tell them I don't get blisters anymore. They tell me that I should be careful and not do long days in the heat with my EB. I tell them I don't have that anymore, and they, too, could follow my protocol, be blister-free, and enjoy all the things I do. You can lead a horse to water... I guess they'd rather do the hard work of suffering than the hard work of getting better.

I celebrated with a bottle of wine and a cigar after that day!

I went to support my wife at a half marathon she was running on Cape Cod. As she was registering at the sign-in desk, I somehow got talked into entering a 10K. I hadn't prepped for it, wasn't wearing athletic shoes or clothing, and didn't eat for success ahead of it. I did it, though. Not a single blister. Lots of muscle pain for a few days, but EB-free!

After about two or three years of not following the protocol, I started back up and began hiking. I was blister-free in about three to five months. The weekend after I hiked Mount Washington, I hiked Mount Katahdin to the summit and back without getting a single blister. These were both long hikes, more than eight hours, while wearing a pack weighing close to sixty pounds. It required a tremendous amount of training and mind control for me to hike the mountain without injury or blisters after just three months of training. The following week, I hiked Mount Monadnock. I could just keep going and going. The protocol works time and time again.

As I search the internet and find really good online EB communities such as Facebook, EB Connect (www.ebconnect. org), etc.—I read many stories about people doing what they want, which I'm sure they considered impossible at one point in their life. I see stories about people who lied about their EB to get into the military or become police officers, firefighters, and emergency management technicians, and they make it through the training. I read about a girl in Austria who has EB and made the cover of a modeling magazine, and she has a tattoo! *Servus Lena! Du bist sehr schön!* (Hello Lena! You are very beautiful). People with EB who get a tattoo have the right mindset—they were probably told not to do it, and they did it anyway. After reading some of the stories out there, mine seem insignificant. I know that is not true. I have paid my price in pain, humiliation, depression, stress, and failure, and I made it through. Hell, I made it ahead. Far ahead. The bottom line is, people with EB can not only do what people without EB can do, but we can also do more if we want to.

If any person decides that they want to follow all or some of this protocol, it is entirely up to the individual, and I would love to hear about the successes as well as the failures. Remember, failure is a big part of the success and steering process. Use all failures as a steering mechanism. When you fail, tell yourself "Good, I can eliminate that product or practice. Now let me try the next one."

SUMMARY

- Build your own list of impossibles and start to make them possible. It is a must-do.
- Create a goal card and carry it with you everywhere. Read it often.
- If you think something is impossible because of EB, take small or large steps toward this goal every day with confidence that you will succeed.
- Celebrate success, study your failures, and adjust accordingly.
- Love yourself at all times. Period.

everydaybeliefs@gmail.com

RESOURCES, REFERENCES AND PRODUCTS

Products I use daily, have experimented with or use as needed to keep me in top form:

Hammer Nutrition – vitamins, electrolyte tablets: I take the daily essentials, tissue rejuvenator, AO Booster, Super Anti Oxidant, Boron, Xobaline, Phytomax. Mention my name and get a nice discount of 10% on your first order. www.hammer-nutrition.com

Snake Diet – Cole Robinson. You can enter his name or Cole Robinson weight loss in YouTube and find plenty of entertaining videos and tutorials to watch.

Udo's 3-6-9 oil – udoerasmus.com

Flora Super 8 Hi-Potency Probiotics – I purchase from www.allstarhealth.com

Gardein – Plant based food. Found in the frozen section of most major grocery chains.

Engine 2 Products - Plant based food. Found in the frozen section of most major grocery chains.

Cetaphil lotion – I purchase on Amazon

Vermont Premium Emu Oil – I purchased at a local farmers market in Massachusetts but you can find a wide variety online.

Skintifique Hydrating Gel – www.skintifique.me

Darn Tough Vermont Socks – www.darntough.com

Good Feet orthotics and inserts – www.mygoodfeet.com

Allbirds – manufacturer of shoes and socks – www.allbirds.com

Giesswein boots – us.geisswein.com

Sperry Shoes – I like the Topsiders boat shoes. www.sperry.com

Timberland Boots – Pro Series. I usually wear the low tops but do have a pair of ankle highs in case the job site requires ankle height boots. www.timberland.com

New Balance – I was fortunate to grow up right next to the factory in Boston. You can get amazing deals if you have the chance to visit the outlet store in Boston. www.newbalance.com

511 tactical pants with knee pads – www.511tactical.com

Desantis duty belts: I have several styles and sizes to help change it up for my skin and for different occasions. www. desantisholster.com

Bottled water – made from 100% spring water: I buy Zephyrhills by the case.

Fresh squeezed orange juice – A full glass in the morning: I buy Natalies by the gallon.

Gillette Safety Razor Company – Fusion Razor System.

Onyx Professional Foot Rasp – CVS/Walgreens or Walmart

The Wim Hof Method – www.wimhofmethod.com

BIBLIOGRAPHY

Innercise: The New Science to Unlock Your Brain's Hidden Power
Doctor, Your Medicine Is Killing Me! by Pete Coussa

Becoming Supernatural: by Dr. Joe Dispenza

Psycho-Cybernetics: by Maxwell Maltz

Thresholds of the Mind: by Bill Harris

Healing the Gerson Way: by Charlotte Gerson

Think and Grow Rich: by Napoleon Hill

Ask: by Mark Victor Hanson

Proctor and Gallagher Institute

Centerpointe Research institute Holosync meditation program. Go to the website for a free sample. www.centerpointe.com

Richard L. Haight's *The Warrior's Meditation: The Best-Kept Secret in Self-Improvement, Cognitive Enhancement, and Stress Relief, Taught by a Master of Four Samurai Arts*

The Mindbody Prescription: Healing the Body, Healing the Pain: by John E. Sarno, MD

The Engine 2 Diet: The Texas Firefighter's 28-Day Save-Your-Life Plan that Lowers Cholesterol and Burns Away the Pounds: by Rip Esselstyn

The JJ Virgin Diet: Drop 7 Foods;Lose 7 Pounds, Just 7 Days

The Gerson Therapy: The Proven Nutritional Program to Fight Cancer and Other Illnesses. 2001.